MASTERING THE ART OF BUSINESS NETWORKING

The Roadmap to Success and Fulfillment

The 8 Essential Steps to Creating Lasting Connections

ISBN: 9798860632011

Acknowledgments

It has been an incredible adventure writing this book, "Mastering the Art of Business Networking," and I am profoundly appreciative of the countless people and institutions who have helped and inspired me along the way. As I share this book, I want to extend my heartfelt gratitude to those who have contributed to the realization of this project.

My deepest gratitude goes out to the innumerable businesspeople, entrepreneurs, and teachers that I've met and learned from throughout the years. The ideas in this book would not exist without your insight and willingness to share your knowledge.

To my friends and coworkers, I truly appreciate hearing about your own business networking experiences. Thank you all for your contributions and insights, this book reflects the broad diversity of the corporate networking environment.

To my family, Aun, Christian, and Christa, your endless support has been the backbone of this project. Your unending support, tolerance, and faith in my projects have been indispensable to me. Without your unwavering encouragement every day, I would never have started and completed this book.

Last but not least, to those who are supporting this book, I want to say how grateful I am for your interest and time. My purpose in writing this book is to provide you with the knowledge and tools you need to build meaningful connections and realize your networking objectives.

I really do appreciate everyone who has helped me on this fantastic journey. The encouragement and motivation I've received from every single one of you has been invaluable. Thank you for making this possible.

With heartfelt appreciation,

Matthew Lin

Table of Contents

Introduction

Networking is the No. 1 unwritten rule of success in business.
—Sallie Krawcheck, CEO and co-founder of Ellevest

Within the fast-paced world of banking and business, Sallie Krawcheck, former head of Bank of America's Global Wealth and Investment Management division and current CEO and co-founder of Ellevest, is a business leader and visionary who understands that success not only requires knowledge, skills, and talent, but also working relationships with others with whom you can partner on projects, share ideas, and collaborate, summarized in her quote above.

As someone who has worked her way up the Wall Street ladder and is now known as "the most powerful woman on Wall Street," Sallie Krawcheck is a great example of someone who is tenacious, determined, and understands how to get ahead in her career. But her statement makes it clear that her achievements are not just due to her intelligence and hard work, but also her skills and efforts in developing her network and building key relationships. This belief in the power of relationships has shaped her approach to business and management, in which she relies on a strong support system of mentors, peers, and allies.

In fact, according to an interview on The Business Journals website, Sallie Krawcheck's path to purchasing the Ellevate Network all started on a plane ride in 2009, where she met Arthur Levitt, former chairman of the US Securities and Exchange Commission. Levitt later connected her with one of his contacts at Goldman Sachs, who then introduced her to one of his contacts, which led to seven more introductions before

Krawcheck met Janet Hanson, founder of 85 Broads, an organization created to support women in business. Krawcheck then bought 85 Broads from Hanson in 2013 and renamed it Ellevate.

Krawcheck says that the key commonality in all these connections is that they were "loose connections," people who she met and knew of casually, not people who became close relationships. However, these connections should go beyond mere business card exchanges. Krawcheck says she maintained these connections through what we will talk about in the rest of this book, by cultivating authentic connections, keeping in contact in personal, meaningful ways, giving before getting, exchanging valuable knowledge, and providing assistance. In this way, her success was not solely focused on personal advancement, but rather on helping others along the way as well.

As Sallie's became a prominent figure in the financial industry, she also began to use her professional connections not just to further her career, but also to advocate for issues she held dear, promoting the principles of diversity, inclusivity, and ethical conduct within the realm of business. Her ability to establish personal connections with individuals, irrespective of their social standing or other differences, highlights her dedication to fostering inclusivity rather than division, another key element of networking we will discuss in this book.

Further, Sallie encourages others' professional growth, emphasizing the importance of genuine relationships that foster mutual growth and achievement within her network. She motivates individuals to perceive networking not merely as a transactional pursuit, but rather to foster a supportive community.

Sallie's accomplishments through her devotion to authentic, mutually beneficial networking serve as a guide to us as we navigate the intricate landscape business networking, showing that genuine achievement is not attained in seclusion, but rather by fostering a comprehensive and varied network of relationships in which collaborative efforts, shared learning, and mutual evolution can flourish.

MASTERING NETWORKING

As evidenced by Sallie's story, it is clear that mastery of networking is a sure path to business success. As a businessperson, you can think of your professional network as a carefully woven tapestry, with each thread indicating a relationship with the ability to weave new opportunities, partnerships, and insights into the fabric of your professional path.

Your job in creating this valuable network is cultivating meaningful relationships. However, doing so is more than a talent; it is an art form with the capacity to change your destiny, propel your business's growth, and reveal previously unknown possibilities. While many people may see this worthwhile opportunity as a painful, fruitless process, it is likely because they have been approaching it all wrong, as more like a transaction than a relationship. The reality is that when networking is done correctly, it can be uplifting, fulfilling, and transformational for all parties involved.

In this book, *Mastering the Art of Business Networking: The 8 Essential Steps to Creating Lasting Connections*, we will explore the fascinating world of networking, detailing simple yet effective ways to create, nurture, and utilize connections in a way that transcends transactions to create long-term impact for both you and those in your network. We will help you understand the chemistry of human connections, establish a culture of reciprocity, and craft a rich tapestry of relationships that are both authentic and purposeful.

In this thorough guide, we will reveal the blueprint for becoming a master networker, someone who can adeptly negotiate the delicate balance between strategy and sincerity, by sharing the eight crucial actions that will help you handle networking events with confidence, make relationships that will last, and use the aggregate power of your network to fuel your ambitions. The steps we cover are:

1. Step 1: Define Your Networking Objectives
2. Step 2: Create a Genuine Personal Brand
3. Step 3: Develop Your Communication Skills
4. Step 4: Make use of both online and offline platforms.
5. Step 5: Give Before Receiving
6. Step 6: Develop Meaningful Follow-Up
7. Step 7: Embrace Diversity and Inclusion
8. Step 8: Encourage Lifelong Learning and Development

We draw inspiration from prominent business executives, visionaries, and thought leaders and distill their wisdom into actionable ideas to help you along your journey. Each step is a brushstroke on the canvas of your networking masterpiece, illuminating the route to success and helping you capture possibilities that otherwise would have gone unnoticed.

This guide is your compass, leading you through the difficult terrain of connection development with grace and composure, whether you're a seasoned entrepreneur looking to increase your influence or a rising professional attending your first networking event.

As you embark on this enlightening journey of learning the art of business networking, keep in mind that the connections you make are more than just steppingstones—they are bridges to success, doors to knowledge, and conduits for transformation. So with an open heart and an inquisitive mind, let us delve into the eight crucial stages that will equip you to form enduring connections, navigate the maze of opportunities, and sculpt a network that is as meaningful as it is powerful.

STEP 1:

Define Your Networking Objectives

Setting goals is the first step in turning the
invisible into the visible.
—Tony Robbins

Tony Robbins, a famous motivational speaker from Los Angeles who pushes audiences to strive for and achieve their goals, is the inspiration for this chapter on setting goals for networking. One of Tony's biggest strengths is helping people turn their dreams into reality.

In his life, Tony overcame many personal obstacles to success after growing up in a poor neighborhood and experiencing the harshness of the world from a young age. He understands how obstacles, both physical and mental, hold people back from achieving all they can, and he teaches his followers to overcome their obstacles through the power of goal setting.

Tony's story, from his humble beginnings to the influential, wealthy household name he is today, is proof that his belief about the power of goal setting is true. Despite encountering difficulties, he always knew he was meant for something bigger, and instead of focusing on all he didn't have, he focused on the life he wanted.

In his youth, Tony actively pursued mentors and sought guidance from unconventional sources. He avidly read books, went to educational conferences, and listened to the words of successful people from different fields. One of the keys that stuck with him through these experiences is the importance of setting goals to achieve your dreams.

Motivated by this simple revelation, Tony went on a journey of self-exploration and personal development, establishing realistic, attainable, and specific goals for personal advancement. As he started to achieve these goals, he saw firsthand their power in his life, sparking his passion for sharing this wisdom with a wider audience.

Unfortunately, Tony faced a lot of skepticism and doubt early in his career. Critics called his views into question, saying they were just empty words that sounded good but didn't really mean anything. But Tony kept going, as he knew the truth. He saw the connection between people's dreams and actions, and he was determined to help others achieve their goals.

Soon enough, Tony began organizing and leading his own seminars and workshops. That's when things really started to take off for him. His captivating talks and engaging events helped thousands upon thousands of people change their lives and realize their dreams. He based his teaching philosophy on the quote, "Setting goals is the first step in turning the invisible into the visible." He helped people set goals, express their ambitions clearly, and develop practical plans to achieve them.

From that point on, Tony's influence continued to expand. He became so well-known that his name is now practically synonymous with empowerment. His seminars are packed with people from all over the world, eager to hear what he has to say, and his advice in his books and workshops helps countless people every year turn their dreams into reality.

Ultimately, Tony's story is an inspiration to us all, showing the power of the human spirit to overcome adversity. He went from humble beginnings to achieving great things, proving that anything is possible if you set your mind to it. His words will continue to motivate people for generations to come, reminding us that we can achieve anything we set our minds to.

With this great example of the power of goal setting in mind, let's look at how we can apply this to our networking to get the best results in the least amount of time.

SETTING A CLEAR PURPOSE

In anything you do, a clear purpose gives you a set goal to achieve and helps keep you on the path as you take action toward it, and it is no different for business networking. It is just like a painter creating a masterpiece: understanding what the subject of the final painting should be dictates the brushstrokes needed to create the final image.

If you are new to business networking or you haven't quite mastered it yet, you may feel like you don't really know how to get started. It can be difficult to strike up a conversation at stuffy networking events, meet people you believe can be valuable parts of your network, or find events where people will be interested in what your business has to offer. These are all challenges those looking to network may face and more, but setting goals can help you overcome these issues.

In this foundational first step of networking, we detail the art of setting specific networking objectives to transform chance meetings into intentional engagements and aimless wandering into systematic connection-making. We will outline why and how to set networking goals, and then we will provide six clear steps to help you get started.

WHY YOU SHOULD SET NETWORKING GOALS

Defining your networking objectives, like setting sail with a destination in mind, enables you to create connections with aim and direction. It gives you something concrete to work toward and helps keep you motivated and accountable for reaching those goals.

There are several reasons why setting networking goals is important for effective networking. Setting networking goals will help push you toward meeting new people and making meaningful connections, give you direction and a sense of purpose in your daily work activities, and keep you focused so you can achieve the important goal of building a network. Having set goals and writing them down will also help you stick to the activity of networking longer, even amid setback, and will make your networking more productive, as it will be a priority.

In the end, all of these factors help lead you to your main goal in your business, becoming more profitable and sustaining success into the future.

SETTING SMART NETWORKING GOALS

When setting your networking goals, it can be helpful to use the SMART approach to goal setting, which you likely have heard about or used at some point in your business career. SMART goals are Specific, Measurable, Attainable, Relevant, and Timebound:

Specific: Tell exactly what you want to achieve. Make it as specific as possible. E.g., "I want to create three new connections with CEOs in my industry this month."

Measurable: Make sure that what you want to achieve can be tracked or measured in some way, and decide how you will measure it. A good way to do this for networking is setting a number of new contacts per year, month, week, event, etc.

Attainable: Make your goal realistic. It should be hard enough that you are motivated to work for it but not so hard that you know you will never reach it and get discouraged.

Relevant: Make sure the specific goals you set are relevant to your overall business goals. You don't need to make three new local business contacts if you are trying to expand your business overseas, for example.

Timebound: Do you want to achieve this goal this week, this month, in six months, or in a year, etc.? Give yourself an exact date for the deadline, so you can easily see if you have met your goal. Whether you meet your goal or not, at the deadline, you can set a new one and try again.

6 EFFECTIVE STEPS FOR SETTING NETWORKING GOALS

Now let's get into the details of actually setting your goals. There are six simple steps to follow, as listed below:

1. **Define What Networking Success Will Look Like**

   What are you looking to achieve with your network? You need to know your why or whys for networking, so you can target the right people in the right places. Some of the reasons you may want to network are as follows:

   - To get more referrals
   - To create more awareness for your business
   - To partner with other businesses for cross-marketing or collaborating on a product or service
   - To create new contacts for sourcing
   - To establish business relationships with potential customers or customers
   - To find a mentor or mentee
   - To find or create a mastermind group
   - To break into new industries or markets
   - Others

   Take a look at this list and decide which of these things are important to you. Write them down or type them out, and then prioritize them from most important to least important. Finally, decide how many hours per week you have to devote overall to networking. Then divide that among the reasons so you can see how much time per week you will spend on each. The amount of time should be the highest for the most important task and the lowest for the least important task.

2. **Review Your Current List of Connections**

Next, you should review your current list of contacts. If you're like most people, you probably already have a list of contacts whose network you already use in some way. Review this list and determine which contacts can help you achieve the networking goals you listed in the previous section.

Again, list the names and rank them from least to most helpful in terms of growing your network. If some people can only be used for certain goals, note that next to their names. When you are ready to get started with networking, you will contact the person highest on the list first.

3. **List the Connections You Want to Make**

Networking takes considerable commitment and effort, so it is important to focus on the connections most important for reaching your business goals. Figure out who you want to connect with, what they can help you do, and what kind of relationship you want to have with them. Also ask what you want to learn about these people and how you can create a good relationship with them.

These people can be from your current network, but you are now going to become more intentional about creating a relationship with them, or they could be the connections of people in your network.

Knowing the people you want to network with will help you decide what types of networking activities you will focus on. There may be certain events where you can meet new contacts, or you may take a previous contact out to lunch to start rekindling the relationship, for example.

4. **Make an Actionable Plan**

   Now that you know who you want to meet, you can make an actionable plan for doing so.

   Set some goals here, both short-term and long-term, and start taking action toward them. The goals may be things like the following:

- Connecting with ten new people a week on LinkedIn
- Emailing ten new people each week
- Meeting two to five new people each week
- Talking to a new person each day either online or on the phone
- Taking one person to lunch each week
- Going to a networking event each month
- Going to industry events once or twice a year
- Others

   Plan around what works best for your schedule and personality so you can realistically achieve it. Ensure you set aside time specifically for networking activities each day or week, so they don't get put to the side when "more important" things come up.

5. **Strategize Your Approach in Advance**

   Think about how you want to present yourself as you begin your networking journey. Do you want to position yourself as a thought leader in your business, sharing your views and experience with others? Do you want to broaden your business's reach and attract new clients or colleagues? Or do you want to be a change agent, bringing together like-minded people to launch influential projects or initiatives? What you decide here will influence where and how you interact with those you want to network with.

You can then take these major goals and break them into smaller, actionable plans. For example, if you want to create mentorship connections, choose industry leaders you like and plan to reach out to them in a strategic way.

As you start to implement your networking plan, there are a couple of other key things to keep in mind. Number one, go into your networking with the thought of helping others. In this way, you can create reciprocal relationships in which you each help each other. You can also get ideas from others. See what other people are doing or even ask them to get good ideas for networking. Finally, maintain flexibility with your goals, seeing networking as a journey, not a race. As you progress in your networking, you may encounter unforeseen changes that force you to change direction. By remaining adaptable, you may seize these unexpected opportunities without losing sight of your overall goals.

6. **Track Your Progress**

We suggest tracking contacts so you can keep up with contact information, set reminders for keeping in touch, and see how much success you are having with certain methods of networking.

Tracking Contact Information

As you start to make new contacts, it is important to keep their contact information organized so you can find it and use it again. This can be as simple as using an Excel spreadsheet or as complex as using something like Clay or another CRM to keep track of contacts' information and conversations, analyze contacts by industry and location among other factors, and set reminders for keeping in touch or even sending automatic messages from time to time.

Measuring Success

Creating metrics to track your progress is an important part of reaching your networking goals. How will you know if you've met your objectives? Is it based on the number of relevant connections you've made, the quality of the collaborations you've launched, or the information you've learned from industry experts? By defining your metrics for measuring success, you set a yardstick for tracking your progress and adjusting your plan over time. You may also find that one tool works better than another at building rapport or getting leads.

Using Tony Robbins's advice, imagine your ambitions as beacons illuminating the route to your dreams. You're not merely participating in random conversations with each step you take—you're embarking on a purposeful quest, weaving connections that add to the big tapestry of your professional path.

KEY TAKEAWAYS:

1. Defining your networking goals allows you to have clarity and direction in your networking activities, allowing you to make informed decisions, prioritize connections, and customize your approach to each networking opportunity.

2. Having clear and SMART networking goals gives you motivation to keep going when the going gets tough during your networking efforts.

3. Through your goals, you can determine which relationships are most important and how you can most effectively obtain them.

4. With your carefully created networking strategy, you can build an intentional network in which you create win-win situations with your connections and continue to build and grow your business into the future.

5. Remember to track your progress to see what works and what does not, as well as to keep up with your new contacts and what you have discussed. This will allow you to adapt as needed and continue to tweak your approach.

As you progress in the world of business networking, keep in mind that setting goals is a continuous process. Goals may change as your career grows, so revisit and improve them on a regular basis to ensure they remain relevant. By utilizing the power of purpose, you are setting yourself up for a networking journey that is not only fulfilling but also primed for extraordinary success.

In the next chapters, you'll learn how each subsequent step connects to your goals, forming a framework for mastering the art of business networking. With your networking goals in place, you're ready to dive deeper into networking, learning how to create a personal brand that represents the authentic you in the best possible light.

STEP 2:

Create a Genuine Personal Brand

Your brand is what people say about you
when you're not in the room.
—*Jeff Bezos*

Jeff Bezos, founder and executive chairman of Amazon, is a business visionary who set out to revolutionize the global shopping landscape. He wasn't satisfied with just creating a successful business; he wanted to build a brand that would last forever. His desire to create a strong brand presence that left a lasting impression on people was realized with the creation of Amazon, and his journey and the essence of his brand is well captured in his statement: "Your brand is what people say about you when you're not in the room."

Jeff's journey to create Amazon started with a simple idea to create a digital platform where people could buy anything from books to electronics and have it delivered right to their door, offering a level of convenience never before seen. This idea, coupled with Jeff's commitment to creating a strong brand that people couldn't forget turned into the massive e-commerce company we know as Amazon today.

As Amazon grew, Jeff Bezos became more and more aware of how important reputation is. He realized that a brand is more than just a logo or a slogan—it's the sum total of every customer's interaction with your company. That reputation extends beyond your own walls to include the conversations people have about you when you're not around—the whispers, the endorsements, and the opinions that shape people's perceptions of your brand.

Jeff Bezos had a clear vision of what he wanted Amazon to be and the reputation he wanted it to have, so he set high standards for customer service and created a seamless, intuitive customer journey. He also created an environment where employees were encouraged to be creative and take risks. Bezos understood that every decision, big or small, would contribute to Amazon's reputation.

Jeff's quote, "Your brand is what people say about you when you're not in the room," was the motto that guided his vision, and he placed a high value on authenticity versus making hollow commitments, and concentrated on cultivating enduring connections rather than pursuing immediate benefits. He wanted people to speak favorably about Amazon in his absence, and he knew that to make that happen, the company had to continually surpass expectations and provide outstanding value.

As we all know, Amazon became a big player in the market because they always put the customer first. Every new program they rolled out, like Prime and their recommendation algorithms, was all about making things easier and more convenient for customers. Jeff Bezos, understanding the true value of branding, knew that it wasn't just about the product or the logo, but about the emotional connection people had with the brand. He knew that people loved Amazon because it made their lives easier, and he made sure that was reflected in everything Amazon did.

Jeff Bezos's vision has transformed the online shopping experience with his development of Amazon. When you see the Amazon logo, you see not only a symbol of modern commerce and customer-centricity, but also the arrow/smile that is the true focus of the brand, delivering smiles around the world.

Jeff's vision and leadership in the business world has greatly impacted the way people think about brands. Entrepreneurs and businesses of all sizes took notice of his words and started to see brands as living, breathing things that are shaped by the business's actions, values, and relationships. Jeff's legacy is a reminder that true success is about more than just money; it's about the lasting impact a brand can have on people's emotions and thoughts.

Jeff's dedication to building a brand that is spoken of with respect even when he's not around has not only changed the way people shop around the world but has also paved the way for a new era of commerce. In this new era, a brand's reputation is just as important as its products, and success is measured not only by financial gain, but also by the lasting admiration of customers.

Throughout the rest of this chapter, let's take a page from Jeff Bezos's book to see how you can create a personal brand that creates a lasting image in people's minds like Amazon has.

WHAT IS YOUR PERSONAL BRAND?

The world of business networking is undoubtedly fast paced, your personal brand is the authentic image you bring to the world, with the capacity to fascinate, inspire, and leave a lasting impression, distinguishing you from the masses of other professionals in the same way that a characteristic tune identifies a composer. In this chapter, we delve into the art of creating a personal brand. In this crucial part of networking, you'll develop a narrative that transcends resumes and business cards, encouraging others to want to connect with you.

To start, let's define the term *personal brand*. Your personal brand is an authentic expression of who you are, what you stand for, and the value you bring to the table. Your personal brand includes things like your values, experiences, and knowledge that resonate sincerely with and leave a lasting impression on those with whom you connect.

You shape your personal brand by making purposeful decisions in your communication style, internet presence, and even clothes—all the ways people perceive who you are. You can craft it consciously to create a consistent narrative about you that piques interest and encourages engagement. There are several considerations when developing your personal brand, which we will discuss in the rest of this chapter.

DISPLAYING YOUR INDIVIDUALITY

First up is displaying your individuality. Self-discovery—an introspective look into your passions, strengths, and values—is at the heart of this step. What do you want people to think about when they hear your name? What are your guiding principles? What distinguishing characteristics do you have? What role do you see yourself playing in your industry or field?

Remember that authenticity is key here. Your personal brand should accurately reflect who you are and resonate with your true self. The more genuine your brand, the more magnetic its pull, as it serves as a beacon to attract people who share your beliefs and goals.

CRAFTING YOUR BRAND NARRATIVE

Now that you have an idea of what you want your personal brand to be about, it's time to create a compelling, snappy narrative that concisely states your path, accomplishments, and future goals. This "story" acts as the introduction to your networking connections, presenting you in a way that piques their interest and encourages greater engagement.

In essence, this should be like an elevator pitch, a short statement that delivers the essence of your brand quickly, one you could say to someone in the time it takes to take an elevator ride. This succinct, effective introduction should encompass your professional identity, your distinctive abilities, and the value you bring to the table. Use this brand narrative to create the groundwork for meaningful connections, whether at networking events or through digital interactions. People form opinions about you within about ten seconds of meeting you, so by crafting this statement, you can help shape their opinions.

CONSISTENCY ACROSS PLATFORMS

In this digital age, your personal brand goes beyond face-to-face interactions and extends to online platforms. This means that creating a cohesive and memorable brand requires consistency on all channels, online and off. Every touchpoint, from your LinkedIn page and social media presence to your in-person presence at events and offline advertising, should reflect the same essence—the true image that you've painstakingly developed.

FOSTERING LASTING IMPRESSIONS

As you embark on your networking journey, remember that the impressions you leave are like brushstrokes on a canvas, each one painting the masterpiece of your personal brand. Every interaction, email engagement, and handshake should convey the values and characteristics of your brand.

According to Jeff Bezos, your personal brand is more than simply a label—it's a dynamic force that connects with sincerity. You're not just introducing yourself when you master the art of establishing an authentic personal brand; you're inviting others to join you on a path of shared values, mutual progress, and lasting connections.

Make the most of both the offline and digital landscape to demonstrate your knowledge, offer your thoughts, and engage in relevant dialogue. Doing this will establish you as a dependable source of value within your network, strengthening your personal brand.

Finally, remember that personal branding is a live, ongoing activity, not a static endeavor. As you gain experiences and insights, you will continue to improve and enhance your brand, much like an artist does with their method. By regularly developing and improving your personal brand, you build a reputation that precedes you, producing a magnetic force that attracts meaningful connections to you.

KEY TAKEAWAYS

1. "Your brand is what people say about you when you're not in the room," says Jeff Bezos. This is a good reminder that the essence of your personal brand creates a lasting impression.

2. Craft your personal brand with your values, strengths, and aspirations in mind to develop a distinctive brand image that is unmistakably yours. Your authentic brand will act as a beacon to other like-minded people, drawing them to your story, expertise, and ambition.

3. Create an elevator pitch as a brief yet powerful description of your personal brand to capture your audience's attention and foster deeper interactions.

4. Maintain consistency across online and offline platforms to flawlessly reflect your personal brand across all channels.

5. Become a trusted source that your network goes to for insights, inspiration, and collaboration, through carefully curated material, smart interactions, and a consistent voice.

As we wrap up this chapter, keep in mind that your personal brand is a live entity that evolves as you do. Your brand narrative grows and becomes deeper as you gain more experience and expand within your area, much like an artist's style matures with time.

Now that you understand the intricacies of creating a personal brand, in the next chapter, we will discuss developing good communication skills to foster a genuine exchange of ideas, insights, and understanding in your network.

STEP 3:

Develop Your Communication Skills

The most important thing in communication
is hearing what isn't said.
—Peter Drucker

Peter Drucker was a widely-known, influential author on the subject of management. This brilliant thinker's ideas profoundly changed the way we understand management and leadership, with his insights that went far beyond the walls of academia and into the realm of interpersonal relationships, as summed up by his famous quote: "The most important thing in communication is hearing what isn't said."

Peter, driven by a desire to understand the complexities of organizations and the people who run them, immersed himself in the world of business and management. Here, he realized the importance of effective communication in achieving business success, but he also understood that the real heart of communication is often in the nonverbal signals, the small gestures, facial expressions, and postures that reveal a deeper meaning than words alone can.

With this realization, Peter dedicated his life to understanding human communication. He studied nonverbal communication, carefully observing social interactions and paying attention to not only what people said, but also how they said it. He realized that subtle nonverbal cues like a raised eyebrow, a brief pause, or a prolonged stare, can convey a lot of information.

Peter wrote that the key to effective communication is to pay attention to the non-verbal cues so you can figure out what people are really thinking, feeling, and wanting. He also believed good leaders and managers need to be good listeners, not just good talkers, and be able to pick up on the non-verbal cues.

Eventually, Peter's theories became well-known, making him a pioneer in the field of management theory. He challenged traditional ideas and proposed new concepts that emphasized the importance of human behavior in the workplace. His ideas stressed the importance of empathy, active listening, and understanding people in the business world.

However, Peter's philosophy went way beyond business and could be applied to many areas of life. His discoveries resonated with and aided people of all types who wanted to build strong relationships, both personally and professionally.

During his lifetime, Peter Drucker helped many people with the books he wrote and the lectures he gave, But his impact was even bigger than that. Because he knew the art of effective communication, he was a master at understanding and connecting with people and was an inspiration to others to learn to listen actively, not just hear, to communicate more deeply with others.

As we dwell on the inspiration that Peter brought to the realm of not only business relationships but personal ones as well, let's see how we can use the concepts of active listening to develop a stronger network through more effective communication.

EFFECTIVE COMMUNICATION

Communication can be thought of as the loom in the big tapestry of business networking, where relationships are the threads that weave success through interaction. Developing good communication skills, like a talented weaver, enables you to establish connections that resonate, inspire, and endure. In this crucial step, we cover the art of communication—an art that goes beyond words and gestures, transforming networking from a transaction into a genuine exchange of ideas, insights, and understanding through effective communication, active listening, articulation, empathy, and non-verbal communication.

Effective communication means connecting with your network's hearts and minds on a deeper level. It's not just about speaking; it's about communicating your thoughts and objectives clearly, with a focus on your audience's needs and with impact. When you communicate effectively, you wield the conductor's baton of communication to arrange engagements that resonate honestly, much as a conductor conducts an orchestra to achieve harmony.

Your communication skills lay the groundwork for long-term partnerships, from active listening that demonstrates genuine interest, to precise articulation of your thoughts. They allow you to communicate your values, share your expertise, and create rapport—all of which are necessary skills for navigating the complex world of networking.

No matter what your communication skills are now, know that they do not remain static; they improve with practice and intention. By honing your communication abilities, you can network with sincerity, respect, and powerful engagement, using both your words and presence to create lasting, beneficial relationships.

Effective communication is not only the words you say, but the art of connecting on a human level, picking up on nonverbal signs, and cultivating a relationship that goes beyond the transactional. It is a two-way street—a harmonious dance in which you express yourself with clarity and delicacy while encouraging others to do the same.

In the next sections, you'll learn how to improve communication in a variety of ways to transform your encounters and relationships.

ACTIVE LISTENING: THE FOUNDATION OF CONNECTION

The technique of active listening—engaging in conversations with a presence that extends beyond words—is at the foundation of good communication skills. Active listening involves providing a safe environment for others to express their thoughts, feelings, and insights because you are listening to understand, not formulating what you are going to say in your head while the other person is speaking. By totally immersing yourself in the conversation, you not only absorb the words said but also pick up on subtle non-spoken cues of certain emotions and points of view.

By being an active listener, you create a bridge to others, allowing you to form true connections based on empathy and understanding. You establish the stage for a more profound and lasting connection by respecting their points of view and expressing that you actually value what they have to say.

ARTICULATION: TRANSFORMING IDEAS INTO MEANINGFUL CONVERSATIONS

Just like a composer arranges musical notes to create a melodious masterpiece, you can carefully articulate your words to poignantly portray your ideas, experiences, and insights to more effectively connect with your network.

To be an effective communicator, practice articulating your thoughts concisely, whether in person or through written communication. Don't take up more of your audience's time than necessary, as it is important to listen more than you speak. Think quality over quantity. An articulate speaker draws attention, piques curiosity, and fosters a respectful environment without hijacking the conversation or boring the audience by talking too much. By eloquently weaving your narrative, you ensure that your message resonates with and is accepted by your audience, creating a lasting impression on them.

EMPATHY: THE CONNECTION'S SECRET SAUCE

Empathy is your secret networking weapon—a skill that allows you to put yourself in the shoes of others and comprehend their viewpoints, motives, and desires. In the same way that an artist analyzes light and shadow to capture the essence of a subject, cultivating empathy allows you to appreciate the complexities of human interactions and build bonds based on shared understanding.

When you approach conversations with true empathy, you foster a culture of trust. Others will feel heard, valued, and respected, paving the path for deeper and more genuine connections. Empathy not only enhances networking contacts, but it also contributes to a culture of collaboration and mutual support.

THE UNSPOKEN LANGUAGE: MASTERING NONVERBAL COMMUNICATION

Nonverbal cues, such as a head tilt, voice modulation, or the warmth of a smile, transmit messages that frequently speak louder than words when building your network. Mastering nonverbal communication allows you to build a dynamic and complex discourse for your listeners' senses, just as a talented artist utilizes brushstrokes to portray emotion.

To enhance your body language, take note of your tone of voice, facial expression, posture, and gestures to ensure they are consistent with the message you are sending. To promote open conversation and present yourself as a likable person, good eye contact, a genuine smile, an upright, open posture with your hands to your side or behind your back, and subtle hand movements instead of keeping your arms stiffly by your side express confidence and openness. But most importantly, don't fake your body language. Make sure it is authentic and matches what you are really feeling. People subconsciously notice if your body language and what you are saying don't match, and they get a sense that something is off. Consistency in your nonverbal and verbal communication will promote a climate of trust and openness, thus strengthening your relationships.

KEY TAKEAWAYS

1. Actively listening, listening by being fully present and not formulating a response in your head while the other person speaks, helps you close the emotional distance between you and your connection.

2. Fully immersing yourself in a conversation to uncover shared opinions, thoughts, and experiences encourages the other person to share their thoughts, dreams, and ideas. This will help you connect with people in your network at a profoundly deep level.

3. Articulation, or the ability to speak with deftness and precision, helps you easily and concisely share your thoughts and ideas, get your connection's attention, and make your encounters not only memorable but also highly influential.

4. Using empathy and putting yourself in the shoes of someone else so you can really understand their point of view allows you to cultivate a safe place for vulnerability, meaningful connections, trust, and understanding within your network.

5. Nonverbal communication, or the unspoken language of gestures, facial expressions, posture, and tone, should be consistent with what you are saying. Your mastery of this strengthens your communication, allowing you to deepen connections and better resonate with your network.

As you progress in your networking career, keep in mind that these improved communication skills are more than just tools; they are the keys that unlock doors to long-term contacts, partnerships, and opportunities. The following chapters will integrate these abilities into a broader framework of networking, directing you toward encounters that are more than just transactions, but experiences of shared meaning and purpose.

As we close the book on the third phase in mastering the art of business networking—cultivating your communication skills—we are now ready to discuss networking through both online and offline platforms.

STEP 4:

Make Use of Both Online and Offline Platforms

Social media is not just an activity; it is an investment of valuable time and resources.
—*Sean Gardner*

Sean Gardner, the author of *The Road to Social Media Success* and undisputed social media guru, having worked with companies like Apple, Microsoft, Marriot, Ford, World Vision, and *The Huffington Post*, among others, is a pioneer in social media who understood its potential to change the world. Sean's insights are summed up in his powerful statement: "Social media is not just something you do; it's an investment of your time and energy."

Sean has always been fascinated by how technology can overcome geographical distances and improve understanding. With the advent of social media platforms, he saw their true potential to be a lot more than just places to share photos, post status updates, and pass the time. He saw a medium for discussion, interaction, and change, a place where voices could be amplified and communities could be formed across borders.

With this realization and a passion to leverage social media for something greater, Sean set out on a purposeful exploration of the world of social media, using the platforms not just for fun, but as tools that could change industries, transform society, and build brands. He understood that success in the digital world required more than just well-written articles. It required a strategic approach and a dedicated investment of time, effort, and resources.

Sean Gardner believes that every tweet, post, and interaction is an important part of a bigger picture that can open doors of opportunity, build relationships, and spread ideas. He sees social media as a tool that can help people share important messages with a wide audience to influence the world.

After sharing his ideas, Sean found many organizations wanted his expertise in navigating the complex world of the internet, while individuals wanted his insights on personal branding and influence. He had a broad perspective that went beyond just numbers, understanding that true value comes from building genuine relationships, starting meaningful conversations, and creating lasting impact.

As Sean's sphere of influence expanded, his commitment to using social media in a socially responsible way also deepened. He advocated for people and businesses alike to use these platforms to promote positive societal impact, to transform the world by amplifying marginalized voices and creating a sense of inclusion around the world.

During a time when we are experiencing an overwhelming influx of information, Sean's approach stood apart from the rest. He adopted the approach of quality over quantity and depth over superficiality. Sean believes that dedicating time and resources toward creating meaningful content and cultivating authentic relationships will result in long-term benefits far more beneficial than simple likes and shares.

Over time, Sean's deep knowledge and understanding of social media has become a guiding light for individuals and brands trying to navigate the complex digital world. His words are a reminder that social media is not just a fun way to pass the time, but a powerful tool that requires purpose, dedication, and a thorough understanding of its capabilities.

Sean's journey to thoroughly understand the power of social media was an important one, and his influence on social media only grew as it continued. His words have had a lasting impact, and they're a testament to his legacy. In a world full of noise, Sean has always emphasized the power of social media to connect people and share ideas. He believes that social media is a powerful tool, but it's important to use it wisely. If you're intentional about it, social media can be a force for good.

Now, with Sean's words of wisdom in our ears, let's explore the details of how we can leverage social media today to aid in our networking efforts.

NETWORKING OPTIONS TODAY

Today, opportunities to connect are no longer limited to physical venues in the ever-expanding environment of business networking. The networking symphony has grown, encompassing both online and offline platforms as instruments—an ensemble that works together to produce a varied song of connections. In this dynamic stage, we explore the art of exploiting both virtual and physical environments—expanding your networking reach and allowing you to engage across geographical boundaries.

Networking in today's world requires expertise in both the digital and physical realms. No longer is networking done only in conference rooms and at chamber of commerce events. Though those things can't be discounted, the virtual realms of social media, online forums, and digital gatherings are just as important if not more. If you don't currently use both or even one of these avenues, it is time to start finding ways to employ them both.

By combining online and physical platforms, you can build connections through things like live networking events, forums, blogs, videos, or social media pages online, or you can talk face-to-face at live events you attend or speak at. This flexibility will allow you to reach a wider and more varied audience, perhaps across several different age groups.

The merging of physical and digital realms presents unlimited prospects for business networking that the world has not experienced before. The convergence of online and offline platforms has changed the art of connection, from virtual forums that span continents to face-to-face meetings that transcend screens. However, to build a strong network, the key is to balance the wide range and flexibility of the online world with the more tangible richness of in-person connections in the offline world.

THE DIGITAL ODYSSEY: HOW TO USE ONLINE PLATFORMS

Today, the world is more connected than ever, and social media is new the town square where ideas, experiences, and relationships are easily traded or shared across a variety of people from all over the world. That means that your online presence has to be more than simply a virtual business card telling who you are. In its most powerful form, you can use it as a channel to broaden your influence, engage with a varied audience, and demonstrate your skills as an expert in your field.

Further, LinkedIn, Twitter, and Instagram are more than just tools; they are virtual stages where your personal brand can shine. You can establish yourself as a thought leader on these platforms—a go-to resource in your industry—by curating insightful content, engaging in important conversations, and sharing your thoughts. The digital image you create for yourself is a beacon that draws like-minded people, generating dialogues and establishing global relationships.

THE TANGIBLE CONNECTION: NURTURING RELATIONSHIPS OFFLINE

While the internet arena has limitless reach, the value of face-to-face contact is unrivaled. Attending conferences, seminars, workshops, and industry events creates opportunities for true connections to form. These events allow you to give your internet contacts a physical touch, where virtual ties become real-life bonds.

When you network in person, you're more than just a name on a screen; you're a real incarnation of your personal brand—a storyteller, an expert, and a collaborator. The art of eye contact, a solid handshake, and real laughter allows you to connect with people more deeply, human to human, which is still important in today's world.

SEAMLESS BLENDING: A SYMBIOTIC APPROACH

As you can probably guess, the best approach is to combine the two forms and network both online and off. Your networking approach will be most effective when you effortlessly mix online and offline networking. To make this work, your online presence should serve as a prologue to in-person interactions, sparking interest and preparing people for meaningful dialogues, as well as allowing you to keep in contact almost daily, with little effort. Similarly, your offline interactions give life to your digital contacts, imbuing them with authenticity and depth when you finally meet someone in real life.

Remember that sincerity is essential on both platforms as you negotiate this contradictory landscape. Whether you're writing a great LinkedIn post or engaging in a conference hallway conversation, your personal brand should be consistent, not leaving room for doubt or questioning your authenticity. Individuals you meet online should recognize you as the same genuine person when you meet in person, and vice versa.

Key Takeaways

1. Both online and offline platforms are equally important for networking today.

2. The digital landscape is a potent stage for spreading your influence and showing your knowledge to a wide range of people all across the globe. Your online presence is more than just a profile; it's a living representation of your personal brand, where you can share useful information, engage in thought-provoking debates, and position yourself as a thought leader.

3. The tangible realm of offline contacts, on the other hand, has its own appeal. Attending events, conferences, and workshops provides a healthy foundation for genuine connections to grow and thrive. You can create rapport that resonates on a truly human level through handshakes, talks, and shared experiences—transcending the confines of digital platforms.

4. By creating a seamless image across both online and offline platforms, you can reach a varied audience and enhance their experiences with you both online and off. Your online interactions set the stage for in-person interactions, while your in-person interactions breathe life into your online relationships, infusing them with authenticity and depth. By being authentic on both platforms and creating a consistent image across them, you will create a beacon for like-minded individuals who will want to become part of your network.

5. As you progress, remember that leveraging online and offline platforms is about orchestrating a perfect blend, not choosing one over the other. Your personal brand should shine through

in both domains, generating a magnetic force that reflects honesty and invites true interactions.

The integration of online and offline networking will continue to impact your path in the following chapters, improving your ability to form connections that transcend boundaries and traverse dimensions. By embracing these platforms' duality, you're immersing yourself in a networking ecology that combines the convenience of the digital with the richness of in-person human contact. As you master the ability to combine online and offline platforms, you will be able to build a large, vital, vibrant network deeply anchored in genuine connection—fully leveraging the power of both technology and human contact.

In the next chapter, we will continue talking about deepening our networking relationships by discussing the power of giving without expecting return to create value and mutually beneficial relationships using the rule of reciprocity.

STEP 5:

Give Before Receiving

Help others achieve their dreams, and you will achieve yours.
—Les Brown

Les Brown, a motivational speaker specializing in personal growth and empowerment, has seen firsthand how language and behavior can have a profound impact on people's lives. His own life story is a testament to his philosophy, which he sums up in this quote: "Help others achieve their dreams, and you will achieve yours."

Les Brown's life journey began in the urban center of Miami, Florida, where he was born into a set of circumstances that may have potentially limited the opportunities available to him. Les, who was first classified as "educable mentally retarded," had various challenges that could have impeded his personal development. However, he exhibited an unwavering determination and an intense motivation to reject the restraints put upon him and overcome his situation.

Determined to change his life, Les started working on himself. He read many books, learned from his mentors, and dreamed big. He loved to tell stories, and he was a great speaker, and he was excited about the future, even though he didn't know exactly what it would hold.

From his mentors, Les learned the power of helping others progress in their lives, and this became his life purpose. He realized his personal journey was to be about more than just achieving personal success, and he dedicated himself to helping others overcome their challenges and actively pursue their aspirations. Realizing that his talent to speak could inspire others and give them hope for a better future, he pursued motivational speaking.

Les Brown put it best when he said that helping others achieve their dreams is the best way to achieve your own. He understood that true satisfaction doesn't come from individual accomplishments alone, but also from lifting others up and making a positive impact on their lives. He realized that by helping people reach their goals, he was also laying the foundation for his own success.

Les became a captivating speaker with an engaging stage presence and relatable stories. His messages weren't just empty words; they were based on his own experiences overcoming challenges, showing it is possible to overcome challenges, achieve your goals, and unlock your potential if you have the right mindset.

As Les became more famous, he continued to expand his reach by writing books, giving seminars, and speaking all over the world with a clear goal of helping people believe in themselves, overcome their limitations, and achieve great things.

Les Brown has become a symbol of optimism and potential over the years. His words have inspired countless people to overcome incredible hurdles by believing in their abilities and striving for great things. His quote, "Help others achieve their dreams, and you will achieve yours," has always been a guiding principle for personal development, effective leadership, and empowerment.

Les's story is a great example of how success is not only about personal achievements but about the impact we have on others and the positive changes we make in the world. Les's journey and wisdom continue to inspire us all, and they remind us of the amazing potential we have to help others achieve their dreams. When we do this, we also create a path for our own dreams to come true.

Les's story about putting a focus on helping others gives us a great basis for the rest of this chapter, where we'll detail the concept of giving before receiving to leverage the power of reciprocity in your networking.

RECIPROCITY

In the intricate choreography of corporate networking, the concept of reciprocity emerges as a guiding principle—allowing you to forge deeper connections and willing collaboration by giving first. Embracing the principle of giving before receiving sets the tone for a happy exchange in your network relationships. In this revolutionary step, we discover the rule of reciprocity and the art of generosity—an art that elevates networking from a transactional endeavor to a cycle of goodwill among all parties involved, resulting in true and mutually beneficial partnerships.

The rule of reciprocity is a rule that describes the universal tendency in human beings to feel compelled to reciprocate when given a gift. Based on this rule, we will talk about generously giving within your network so that they naturally open up and want to give back to you, benefiting the network as a whole.

At the core of giving before receiving is the act of providing value, insights, and assistance to others without expecting anything in return. It is the act of lending a hand, sharing expertise, and contributing to the success of individuals in your network without any strings attached. Your genuine kindness and generosity will leave a lasting impression on people that will open their hearts and make them want to help you in return.

Giving not only forges connections based on trust and reciprocity, but it also positions you as a valued resource inside your network. Your willingness to give increases the quality of interactions, transforming networking into a platform for shared progress.

As we explore this notion in more detail in the next few sections, keep in mind that giving is not a transaction; it is a commitment to developing relationships based on goodwill and mutual success. The power of generosity, which includes leading with compassion, giving to others with purpose, and creating a symphony of connections, will enrich the lives of those around you as well as your own.

PLANTING GENEROSITY SEEDS

The principle at the foundation of this stage is that meaningful connections are nourished through acts of kindness, support, and collaboration. You spread the seeds of generosity within your network in the same way a gardener sows seeds in fertile soil, producing an ecosystem where reciprocity thrives. Your desire to help, share insights, and deliver value without expecting anything in return fosters a sense of trust and goodwill. People will naturally be more open to networking and collaborating with you, as well as giving back to help you succeed as well.

By approaching networking with an open heart and a giving spirit, you're also planting the seeds for long-lasting relationships that go beyond surface exchanges. Your acts of kindness serve as the foundation for long-lasting connections, cultivating a network that is more than just transactional and provides mutual support.

CULTIVATING A CULTURE OF RECIPROCITY

The best way to create a culture of reciprocity is to give freely to those in your network. This can include giving away things like your knowledge and time, the contacts in your network, helpful advice, or even goods and services where appropriate. By doing this without asking for or expecting anything in return, you are cultivating a culture of reciprocity. Those who receive from you will naturally want to provide you with more value in return. This creates an environment where value exchange becomes a natural and harmonious rhythm. As you give to others and they give back to you, it results in a support loop that multiplies the effect of your gifts, creating an ongoing cycle of goodwill and collaboration.

Further, when you assist people in their success and growth in some way by giving them what they need to succeed, you create relationships that are more than just economic transactions. Your acts of generosity establish the framework for connections that are authentic and deep, resulting in a network that is resilient in the face of adversity and celebrates common accomplishments.

THE ABUNDANCE TRANSFORMATION

When you embrace the principle of giving before receiving, you experience a transformation of abundance—the realization that the more you give, the more you receive in return. This transformation is more than just monetary gain; it is a mindset shift that helps you recognize the limitless opportunities that surface when you approach networking with compassion.

By sharing your knowledge, lending a helping hand, or connecting people who can benefit from one another, you're not only helping others succeed—you're also broadening your own horizons. The knowledge, ideas, and doors that open as a result of your contributions enrich your personal journey in unexpected and satisfying ways.

KEY TAKEAWAYS

1. Step 5, "Give Before Receiving," reveals the power of selfless giving inside your network in a world dominated by commerce.

2. Your acts of kindness, support, and aid create trust and goodwill within your connections. By lending a helping hand without expecting anything in return, you create an atmosphere of true camaraderie—a space where genuine connections can grow.

3. Your eagerness to offer freely elevates not only your network but also you. By practicing generosity, you create a culture of reciprocity, where your acts of giving encourage others to do the same in return, multiplying the impact of your efforts as they spread across your network.

4. Giving results in a transformation—an evolution of abundance that surpasses material gains. This shift is based on the realization that the more you contribute to the success and growth of others, the more your own journey is enriched.

5. Every act of kindness, every information transfer, and every connection you facilitate becomes an investment in your personal growth and prosperity when viewed through this lens.

In this chapter, you learned how to create connection and a spirit of mutual support and reciprocity in your network, thus creating a strong network that operates with sincerity, camaraderie, and a sense of shared achievement.

In the next chapter, you'll discover the art of the meaningful follow-up to turn casual contacts into lasting relationships.

STEP 6:

Develop Meaningful Follow-Up

Your network is your net worth.
—Porter Gale

Porter Gale is a marketer who understands that the value of your network goes way beyond just having a lot of friends. In her quote, "Your network is your net worth," she is speaking to the power of networking to get better jobs, find new opportunities, and even just enjoy a better quality of life. She understood that your network is more than just the connections you make. To be an effective networker, besides always looking to meet and connect with new people, you also have to nurture your relationships. You never know who might be able to help you out in the future.

Porter has always been a self-described people person. Even as a kid, she knew that relationships were important. They weren't just something you had for fun or to pass the time—they were opportunities to learn and grow. Understanding that the people you surround yourself with could have a big impact on your life both personally and professionally, Porter made sure to cultivate strong relationships with everyone she met. She knew that these relationships would be essential to her success in life.

Throughout her career, Porter realized that while genuine connections are crucial to success, the quality of your network is more important than the quantity. She doesn't just make connections for the sake of making them; she surrounds herself with positive, supportive people who can help her achieve her goals, learn and grow, and just be a better person. She deliberately builds relationships with others by being genuine and helpful and believes that helping others is the best way to build trust and create mutually beneficial relationships. She has found that helping others not only makes her feel good, but also makes the network stronger.

Porter Gale shares her knowledge with people all over the world in a variety of ways, including public speaking, writing, and mentoring, and her idea that relationships are investments resonates strongly with people from all walks of life. Entrepreneurs, professionals, and thought leaders alike have embraced her philosophy, recognizing that the quality of their relationships can have a big impact on their future success.

Porter's legacy became a powerful reminder that true success is linked to the strength of your relationships. Her quote, "Your network is your net worth," has been repeated in conference halls, corporate offices, and coffee shops. As the world changes, her wisdom continues to shine brightly, reminding us that true value comes not from material possessions, but from the relationships we build.

Throughout the rest of this chapter, we will detail how to build deeper, stronger relationships through meaningful follow-up to add value to your network and nurture the seeds of connection.

MEANINGFUL FOLLOW-UP

Follow-up serves as a bridge between your initial contact with a prospective member of your network and creating a lasting relationship in the orchestration of business networking, where connections are the notes, and partnerships construct the song. In this step, we dig into the delicate dance of post-interaction engagement—an art that converts casual conversations into long-lasting ties, providing continuity and value to your network.

Meaningful follow-up is more than a formality in business; it also demonstrates your dedication to developing relationships and your concern for the well-being of your network. By following up with connections you made, you start to grow your connection and encourage it to become something extraordinary. Effective follow-up isn't about getting anything; it's about deepening relationships and showing you support your network. Further, it is not something you do unintentionally. Instead, you should set aside dedicated time for follow-up and then follow through with doing it. It is also not something you do once with a connection. Follow-up is something you will continue to do in your relationships, though it will evolve naturally as the relationship deepens.

In the rest of this chapter, we will give you some ideas for following up with your connections in a way that doesn't feel forced or awkward, so you can keep the momentum of your conversations going, leave a lasting impression, and position yourself as a trusted collaborator within your network. You'll learn to use follow-up to nurture the seeds of your connections and add value to your relationships. By doing so authentically and consistently, you'll create caring, continuing, long-term connections in your business.

NURTURING THE SEEDLINGS OF CONNECTION

The key to this step is realizing that networking is a journey. It takes time to make connections, and after that it takes time and effort to actually develop a lasting relationship. You must build the connections you've formed intentionally interaction after interaction, in the same way a painter paints a picture brushstroke by brushstroke, until you have created a beautiful relationship.

There are several ways you can do this, and it doesn't have to take a lot of time or cost a lot of money. Send a thoughtful email, call, or arrange a coffee date to continue the conversation and develop your connection further. By doing so, you're implying that your original connection was more than just a transaction and was the start of a meaningful journey. Your follow-up demonstrates your sincerity and the importance you place on the relationship.

THE HEARTBEAT OF FOLLOW-UP: ADDING VALUE

Meaningful follow-up is more than just a continuation of the conversation; it's an opportunity to add value to your contacts' lives. Inject your follow-up with insights, ideas, or opportunities that resonate with the contact's goals and aspirations. Your follow-up should make an impression, enhance your contact's experience with you, and remind your contact of the value you bring to the table.

Consider sending them an article relevant to their interests, introducing them to a potential partner, or providing insights into a problem they have mentioned. By doing so, you display your dedication to their achievement and strengthen the foundation of trust you've built.

FOLLOW-UP KEYS: CONSISTENCY AND AUTHENTICITY

Effective follow-up is consistent. It shows your thoughtfulness and commitment to sustaining the relationship. Consistent follow-up allows your connection to feel like you care and that you are there to listen if they need you. You can do this through regular check-ins through emails, texts, or phone calls; sending updates on your business or personal things you discussed with them; and interacting with them on social media sites or in person.

The soul of good follow-up is authenticity. Just like a singer injects genuine emotion into their performance, your follow-up should do the same. With honesty, express thanks, share your own experiences, and celebrate the triumphs of your contacts. Your genuineness will touch people's hearts and leave a lasting impression.

KEY TAKEAWAYS:

1. It is not enough just to connect with someone, even if the initial contact was strong. Just like any other relationship, the relationships in your network have to be nurtured, and this is done through follow-up.

2. Your follow-up enriches the connection you've sparked, infusing it with life, depth, and purpose, strengthening the connection with each interaction.

3. Through your thoughtful follow-up, you display dedication that goes beyond the surface level—a commitment to understanding, support, and partnership.

4. You can also add value to the relationship with follow-up by providing insights, resources, or opportunities based on something the contact told you in your initial meeting. By doing this, you show your commitment to their growth and success and open the door for them to contact you when they need your expertise.

5. You must be consistent and sincere with your follow-up. Your constant check-ins and conversations guide the evolution of your relationships, and your authenticity makes your contact genuinely like you.

As you continue on your networking journey, keep in mind that cultivating meaningful follow-up requires a mindset of dedication to maintaining connections that go beyond initial interactions, and the time you spend doing so will be well worth it when you cultivate long-term, meaningful business relationships.

In the next chapter you will learn about embracing diversity and inclusion to foster an environment in which all people thrive with a feeling of mutual respect and belonging.

STEP 7:

Embrace Diversity and Inclusion

The strength of the team is each individual member. The strength
of each member is the team.
—Phil Jackson

Phil Jackson, the all-time winningest coach in both Chicago Bulls and Los Angeles Lakers basketball franchise history, was a revolutionary figure in the world of sports and leadership. His deep insights helped teams become dynasties and elevated players to legendary status. His wisdom is evident in his quote, "The strength of the team is each individual member. The strength of each member is the team," which emphasizes the importance of each individual member in creating a strong team, as the team is only as strong as its individual members.

Phil Jackson's story started when he was a basketball player, where he learned to make strategic moves and the importance of teamwork. But it was only later, when he became a coach, that he made a significant difference in the world of sports. He realized that true greatness doesn't come from individual brilliance, but from the combined effort of a team.

As Jackson's coaching career continued, he introduced a new way of thinking about basketball. He understood that the key to success was to take advantage of each player's unique skills while also building a strong team spirit. He believed that it wasn't enough just to have a bunch of talented players, and he wanted to create an environment where the team could work together and achieve more than the sum of their individual parts.

A team's success depends on the unique contributions of each member, and Phil Jackson acknowledged that each player has their own unique skills and qualities, but he also believed that it's the team's ability to work together, support each other, and help each other out that really makes a difference.

Phil is known for his coaching philosophy, which is all about achieving exceptional leadership standards. He's really good at getting the best out of his players by understanding their individual motivations and helping them see how their goals fit into the team's goals. He also emphasizes the importance of trust, communication, and understanding each player's role in the team.

Teams thrived under Phil Jackson's coaching. Under his leadership, the Chicago Bulls and the Los Angeles Lakers won several championships, cementing his legacy as one of the greatest coaches in sports history. His success is a testament to his belief in the power of teamwork.

However, Jackson's ideas didn't just impact the sports world. His understanding of the interconnectedness of individuals and teams resonated in other industries too, like business, education, and more. His words motivated leaders to create environments that foster teamwork and camaraderie, where the success of each individual member contributes to the success of the whole.

As Phil's story continued, his legacy became a guiding light for those trying to understand the fundamentals of teamwork and leadership. He said that the power of a team comes from the unique contributions of each individual member. This idea that a team is only as strong as its weakest link is true in any setting, from the locker room to the boardroom to the classroom. As the world changed, his wisdom remained a reminder that striving for excellence is more than just individual achievement; it's about working together as a team.

Relating Phil Jackson's philosophy to mastering the art of business networking, just as he took a diverse group of men with different skills, talents, mindsets, and opinions to create winning teams, so must you include a wide array of people to create a strong network. Throughout the rest of this chapter, we will look at why this is important and how you can do it successfully to create a diverse and inclusive network.

THE DIVERSITY SPECTRUM: AN INCLUSIVE CANVAS

Diversity and inclusion are the threads that weave a tapestry of rich perspectives, experiences, and ideas in business networking, creating a unified network that celebrates individual differences as well as what makes us all the same. In this critical step, we investigate the transforming potential of embracing diversity and inclusion—an art that goes beyond superficial connections to establish an environment in which all perspectives are not only heard, but cherished.

In the next sections we detail creating a culture of diversity and inclusion in your network through empathy, understanding, and collaboration. This step will teach you how to foster an environment in which authenticity and innovation thrive and all people feel connected to a shared purpose.

Diversity is more than just visible differences—it includes a wide range of cultures, ethnicities, experiences, and identities. Within your network, it is important to strive to intentionally include a diverse range of people and celebrate the beauty in each person's differences, as each person can bring a useful new perspective and skill set.

It is also important to practice inclusion, intentionally inviting those who are different from you into your network and creating an environment in which they are not only tolerated, but their voice is heard, valued, and accepted.

Through exposure to varied perspectives, your network will thrive, and those with open minds will experience growth. You build a dynamic, innovative, and forward-thinking network when you celebrate its diversity.

EMPATHY AND UNDERSTANDING

By accepting that diversity and inclusion is an invitation to broaden your horizons and put yourself in the shoes of others to see life from their perspective, you cultivate empathy and understanding to better connect with people from different backgrounds. You also build a foundation of respect and camaraderie with your network by attempting to comprehend the unique challenges, aspirations, and perspectives of others.

This creates an environment where people feel valued for who they are and fosters a bond between network members founded on trust and mutual appreciation.

AMPLIFYING VOICES AND FOSTERING COLLABORATION

By embracing a culture of diversity and inclusion, you transform your networking from a transactional exchange to a meaningful interaction. You can amplify marginalized voices and provide a forum for perspectives that would otherwise go unnoticed in your network to promote unity, collaboration, and mutual growth.

The acceptance of diversity and inclusion opens the door to cross-cultural collaboration. When people from different backgrounds come together, they contribute diverse ideas that can lead to innovation, problem-solving, and groundbreaking collaborations.

To foster collaboration and amplify marginalized or underrepresented voices, create a space for viewpoints that might otherwise go unheard. Doing so will elevate your networking from a commercial activity to a platform for meaningful participation, helping your connections feel valued.

AN UNWAVERING COMMITMENT

As you embark on your networking journey, remember that supporting diversity and inclusion is a commitment that should carry over into all aspects of your business, not just the ones that will benefit you.

When you cultivate an inclusive attitude, you're not just networking, you're establishing a community that embraces the brilliance of diverse perspectives, creating a culture of unity, respect, collaboration, and mutual growth.

KEY TAKEAWAYS:

1. Diversity can include people from different backgrounds and identities as well as points of view. Including a varied range of people in your network not only broadens your personal horizons but also fosters an environment of creativity, innovation, and growth.

2. Inclusion also focuses on making sure every voice is heard, especially those from marginalized or underrepresented groups. By intentionally creating an environment in which people feel respected, heard, and empowered, you create a space where cooperation and innovation thrive.

3. Empathy and understanding allow you to create friendships with those in your network based on respect and mutual admiration. By putting yourself in the shoes of others, you can better understand things from others' perspectives and promote a strong feeling of community.

4. The acceptance of diversity and inclusion elevates networking from a transactional exchange to a meaningful engagement. As a conductor leads an orchestra to create a symphony that transcends individual instruments, you can lead your different network members to harmonize their abilities and create a partnership masterpiece.

5. As you continue your networking journey, keep in mind that the spirit of diversity and inclusion is a dedication to recognizing the beauty of differences and elevating marginalized voices.

By embracing variety and inclusiveness, you cultivate connection within your network based on unity, respect, and mutual growth. You help others in your network grow and expand their horizons by encouraging them to celebrate the differences in others and what they can bring to the table, leveraging it for profitable collaboration for everyone involved.

This brings us to our final step, "Encourage Lifelong Learning in Development," where you will learn the value of not only encouraging others to continually learn and develop themselves personally, but also how to lead them by doing so yourself to enhance the value of your network as a whole.

STEP 8:

Encourage Lifelong Learning and Development

The only thing that is constant is change.
—Heraclitus

In the world of ancient philosophy, where people thought deeply about life's big questions, there was a famous thinker named Heraclitus, who was known for his deep insights. One of the topics he frequently spoke on is the fact that everything is always changing, stating something that's still true today: "The only thing that is constant is change."

Heraclitus lived in the ancient city of Ephesus around 500 BCE. He was a keen observer and used introspection to contemplate the fundamental nature of existence and the forces that shape it. His philosophy was centered on the idea of *flux*, which means that change is not just a temporary thing, but is the fundamental nature of reality.

Heraclitus said that the only thing that stays the same is change. He believed that everything in the universe is always changing, from the tides to the seasons to the way people think, and that is a natural part of life and therefore important to accept.

Heraclitus's philosophical perspective challenged the idea that the world is stable and permanent. However, he saw change not as a disruptive force, but as a natural part of life. His ideas were different from the common beliefs of his time, which encouraged people to think about the meaning of change.

For centuries, Heraclitus's perspective has resonated with intellectuals and knowledge seekers alike, being widely accepted across a range of disciplines, including philosophy, science, and psychology as a principle that can be used as a guiding framework for navigating the complex dynamics of our ever-changing world.

In today's world, where everything seems to be changing at a breakneck pace, the wisdom of Heraclitus is more important than ever. We must learn to accept and embrace change and to see it as an opportunity for growth and development. We can't get too attached to any one thing, because things are always changing. But if we can learn to roll with the punches, we can find new opportunities and experiences that we never would have found if we had stayed stuck in the same old rut. So next time you feel like things are changing too fast, remember Heraclitus's words and try to embrace the change. Be inspired to wholeheartedly accept the cyclical nature of life. Change should not be perceived as a formidable force to be opposed, but rather as an inherent truth that intricately molds the fabric of our being.

In the world of business networking you can adopt Heraclitus's approach to constant change through encouraging lifelong learning and leading your network toward self-improvement and growth by constantly working toward it yourself. We will discuss why this is important and simple ways to foster constant improvement throughout the rest of this chapter.

THE JOURNEY OF LIFELONG LEARNING

Lifelong learning is a journey that moves both you and your network ahead, improving your interactions and expanding your impact. You can enhance your knowledge and expertise to lead within your network in the same way that a conductor refines their talents to lead an orchestra.

At the same time, you can encourage others to continue learning and growing, thus increasing the value of your network. Embracing constant learning in your networks keeps your connections vibrant, relevant, and at the forefront of innovation, and it ensures that your businesses grow and thrive into the future.

In the same way that a scholar goes into the depths of learning, supporting lifelong learning and development allows you to make connections that resound with depth, understanding, and shared progress. In this final step, we delve into the art of encouraging lifelong learning and development—an art that elevates networking from a one-time event to an ongoing symphony of personal and professional development, in which you and your network celebrate each other's ongoing achievements.

Learning is a universal language that crosses gaps, transcends obstacles, and promotes a collaborative culture. It serves as the foundation for strong connections as you share insights, trade experiences, and explore new ideas together. By building a growth-oriented network, you create connections that resonate with your values of progress and shared goals.

Throughout the rest of this chapter, we will detail the power of lifelong learning and development and how you can promote it within your network. This step will teach you how to nurture a curious mentality, encouraging others to seek opportunities for improvement, thus contributing more to the collective knowledge within your network.

This final step of business networking sends us on a voyage of constant growth and learning—a step that reflects Henry Ford's insight, "Anyone who stops learning is old, whether at twenty or eighty." This final stage demonstrates that networking is not a static activity, but rather an evolving dance that reflects the ever-changing environment of industries, technology, and ideas. When you take this step, you engage on a journey of constant self-improvement, establishing yourself as a lifelong learner and a pillar of knowledge within your network and encouraging those in your network to do so as well.

The Search for Knowledge: A Never-Ending Symphony

The realization that learning is not confined to a classroom is at the heart of this step. Instead, learning is a lifelong endeavor that enriches all aspects of your networking experience, for both you and your contacts. By enhancing your abilities, insights, and knowledge through a dedication to continued study and being up-to-date on the newest advancements, trends, and innovations in your business, you and those in your network can foster a sense of relevancy and agility that will set you apart. As each of you elevates, it not only makes your network more valuable, as you collectively have more to bring to the table, but it also improves your business prospects now and into the future.

At its foundation, networking is about making connections that go beyond the surface. When you encourage your network to invest time in expanding their knowledge, and you lead by example by doing the same, you not only help them grow and expand their horizons, but you also continue to give your network an invaluable resource—a trusted advisor who can provide insights, discuss best practices, and provide professional counsel.

Embracing Change and Adaptation

The last networking step is defined by a readiness to embrace change. Encourage your network to be willing to adapt and evolve alongside their industries' shifting currents while maintaining an open mind to new ideas, technologies, and techniques that will enable them to navigate uncharted territory with grace and confidence. This will help them grow as businesspeople, and when you help others with their personal growth and want them to succeed, they will naturally want to help you and see you succeed.

As a leader in your network, you must also embrace change and adapt. To be a valuable leader, you have to understand that members of your network look to you not only for current information but also for your ability to foresee and navigate challenges and change. By being aware of emerging trends and cultivating an attitude of adaptation, you can help keep others in your network afloat by providing insights and advice when troubles arise and inform them of new opportunities for growth in the ever-changing market today.

SHARING UNDERSTANDING AND INSPIRING GROWTH

As you continue your journey of lifelong learning, you are building a treasure of understanding to share with others, not only gathering knowledge for personal advantage. You, like a mentor, become a mentor within your network, motivating growth and cultivating a culture of continual improvement.

You enable your connections to overcome challenges, seize opportunities, and reach their full potential by sharing your ideas, experiences, and lessons gained. Your position as a lifelong student and educator improves your relationships, transforming your networking experience from a series of transactions to a legacy of growth and positive effect.

THE CHANGING SYMPHONY

As you continue your networking journey, keep in mind that the pursuit of lifelong learning and progress is a mindset—an unrelenting dedication to both your and your network's self-improvement and benefit.

You're not merely networking when you choose the road of encouraging continual learning and growth; you're crafting a symphony of personal and professional development—focused on progress, innovation, and positive change. By doing so, you cultivate a network that naturally raises each other up through a spirit of continuous evolution and limitless potential and is defined by its intellectual vigor, mutual support, and commitment to shared success.

The pursuit of knowledge is a lifelong obligation to discovery, expansion, and the never-ending climb toward greatness. Embrace it in your life and in your network and create a culture of development and possibilities.

KEY TAKEAWAYS

1. Being a leader in your network is not only about enhancing your abilities, insights, and knowledge through continual education and development, but it is also about encouraging your network to do the same. By continually improving yourself, you not only improve your life, but the lives of others by bringing more value to the network through your skills and knowledge.

2. By cultivating a network culture of remaining relevant and up-to-date through continuous personal improvement, you shift your networking from transactional to relational, as you sincerely want to see and help others better themselves.

3. The pursuit of knowledge ensures you and your network are at the forefront of changes and shifts in your industries and the market as a whole. You embrace new ideas, technology, and techniques with grace and help light the way for others in the network to do the same.

4. As you cultivate your own development as the leader of your network, you become an inspiration to people around you. Your dedication to lifelong learning spreads across your network, inspiring others to pursue their own journeys for knowledge and personal improvement. You light a flame of interest and fuel a culture of mutual growth by sharing your wisdom, thoughts, and experiences.

5. As you continue on your networking adventure, keep in mind that lifelong learning and growth require commitment— ongoing dedication to embracing the unknown, the inevitable changes and unlimited possibilities that lie ahead. The preceding chapters have guided you through a networking symphony,

where each step has seamlessly merged with the others to produce a symphony of connection, empowerment, and impact within your network.

With this last step, you are ready to create a symphony of continual development by encouraging lifelong learning and growth with the goals of progress, innovation, and good change.

Now it is time to put together everything you have learned in the book so you can start your journey toward mastering the art of business networking.

Putting It All Together

With the conclusion of the 8 Steps to Creating Lasting Connections, you are now on a path that will change your life forever, but only if you decide to take action. The steps included here, when combined, will result in a masterpiece of interpersonal harmony and professional development. With the advice of successful businesspeople at our side, we've mastered the complex dance of networking and uncovered the secret to making connections that last in a world where everything is constantly shifting.

We started at the beginning, with an appreciation for networking's potential, then worked our way up through the nuance of developing genuine, deep connections. We learned to create a symphony of connection that resounds with authenticity, value, and mutual empowerment through the steps of setting clear intentions, cultivating communication skills, leveraging online and offline platforms, giving before receiving, meaningfully following up, embracing diversity and inclusion, and fostering lifelong learning and growth.

The realization that networking is more than a transaction lies at the heart of this symphony, and it is important to understand that what you put into your network determines what you will get out of it. Each intentional act you do to deepen your connections with those in your network should serve to benefit not only you but more importantly, your connections. By approaching your network with care, understanding, and the intention to help them, you will create a harmonized network of resources to share ideas, partner on projects, create new things, and scale greater heights in your businesses.

You are the conductor of your networking journey, and much like a conductor leads an orchestra to create a unified and beautiful piece of music, by bringing thoughtfulness, compassion, and honesty to every exchange, you can foster an environment where people feel inspired to work together toward a common goal.

Keep in mind that building your network is a continual process, a kind of musical composition that gets better with time and more complex as you add new notes. It's up to you to write the tune to your networking symphony aiming for reaching a wide and varied audience and communicating openly and effectively with them on a variety of platforms, showing generosity with your time and knowledge, following-up, and encouraging diversity and personal growth within your network. By reading this book, you have the resources, understanding, and motivation to begin your networking adventure with confidence and competence.

Now it's time to take your place as both conductor and performer on the networking stage, where the symphony of your connections will be shaped by your every move. You're not just making deals when you learn to network effectively; you're composing a symphony of relationships that resounds with genuine worth and long-term impact. So let the symphony begin, and may your experience in networking be a masterpiece that echoes throughout history and leaves an unforgettable impression in the corporate world and beyond.

Quotes From The Book

Networking is the No. 1 unwritten rule of success in business.
—Sallie Krawcheck, CEO and co-founder of Ellevest

Setting goals is the first step in turning the invisible into the visible.
—Tony Robbins

Your brand is what people say about you when you're not in the room.
—Jeff Bezos

The most important thing in communication is hearing what isn't said.
—Peter Drucker

Social media is not just an activity; it is an investment of valuable time and resources.
—Sean Gardner

Help others achieve their dreams, and you will achieve
yours.
—Les Brown

Your network is your net worth.
—Porter Gale

The strength of the team is each individual member.
The strength of each member is the team.
—Phil Jackson

The only thing that is constant is change.
—Heraclitus

End Notes

We've finally reached the end of "Mastering the Art of Business Networking," and I would like to take a moment to thank you for coming along on this journey. Networking is indeed all about building genuine relationships, giving back more than you receive, and making genuine connections with people, sharing information, resources, and opportunities that can benefit everyone involved.

In this book, we've covered a lot of ground regarding the finer points of networking successfully, including creating a genuine personal brand, using digital platforms, and encouraging lifelong learning and development. I hope you've found these ideas helpful and actionable, arming you with the knowledge and perspective to succeed in today's dynamic business networking environment.

Apply the ideas in this book with honesty and compassion in your networking activities. Strive to make a pleasant and long-lasting impression on the people you meet and focus on creating bridges rather than collecting business cards. If you want to get the most out of networking, you need to go into it with an open mind and heart.

Finally, I'd like to leave you with this parting thought: networking isn't something you do once and then stop doing. Keep communicating, keep gaining knowledge, and keep developing. Your professional network is a direct reflection of your abilities and potential; with time and effort, you may become an expert business networker.

I hope your networking efforts bring you happiness and fruitful relationships and remember, "by listening more, you will Learn More."

Matthew Lin

About the Author

Matthew is a design architect and property developer by day and an ardent self-help writer by night. With a robust background in architecture and property development, Matthew brings a unique perspective to his work: combining creativity, business acumen, and a desire to inspire and empower others through his writing. He is also a dedicated proptech enthusiast and enjoys constantly exploring innovative technologies to enhance the real estate industry.

Matthew's varied life experiences have helped shape his fascinating and motivational persona. After studying architecture in Auckland, New Zealand, he spent more than 10 years working as a design architect in Singapore before shifting gears as a property developer in Thailand for the last 15 years. He is currently working to develop an online platform designed to simplify the real estate ecosystem.

Matthew's expertise extends beyond the realms of blueprints, building sites, and technology. Not only has he consulted numerous businesses—offering 1-on-1 coaching services and advice on general business, real estate, and technology—but he has also supported countless experts and amateurs alike as they seek to better understand their respective industries.

Matthew's path is proof of the positive impact that optimism, creativity, and self-assurance can have on one's life. His life's tale is a motivating example of how anyone can achieve his/her goals with the appropriate attitude and the drive to keep plugging away at them. Matthew's story has inspired people of various backgrounds to believe in themselves and their abilities and take risks in pursuit of their goals.

Current Book List:

- 50 Habits of Highly Successful Business Leaders   (2023)
  The Roadmap to Success and Fulfillment

- Mastering the Art Of Business Networking   (2023)
  The 8 Essential Steps to Creating Lasting Connections.

- Mastering Procrastination & Achieve Your Goals   (2023)
  8 Essential Steps to Regain Control of Your Life

Matthew resides in Chiang Mai, Thailand with his wife and two children. You can reach out to him at www.linkedin.com/in/matthew-lin-72061b282. He would love to hear from you!

www.ingramcontent.com/pod-product-compliance
Lightning Source LLC
Chambersburg PA
CBHW062244290526
45794CB00006B/2391